TO MAKE A BOW:

1

2

1 Measure 18" from one end of the ribbon (this will be the tail or streamer of the bow). Pinch between the thumb and finger of your left hand.

2 Make a loop on each side of your hand.

3

4

3 Make two more loops, one on each side of your hand.

4 Make a center loop by bringing the ribbon toward you--up, over and around the thumb.

5

6

5 Make four more loops--two on each side of your hand.

6 Cut off a 4" length of cloth covered wire or chenille stem. Bend in half and insert through the center loops.

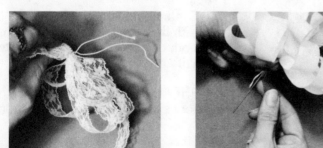

7

8

7 Bring the wire ends to the back of the bow and twist to secure the bow.

8 If necessary, floral tape the bow wires to a 2" piece of 20 gauge wire. Trim the tails of the bow at an angle.

1

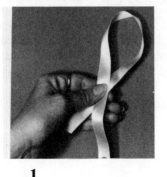

1

2

3

4

5

6

7

8

MANY RIBBONED BOW:
(see page 6, step 9 for the finished product)

1 With the first ribbon make a 4" long loop on one side of your hand.

2 Make a 4" loop on the other side of your hand.

3 Make additional loops on each side of your hand until there are a total of 4 to 10. Cut the ribbon.

4 With the next ribbon or lace make loops on each side of your hand. Notice these loops are slightly smaller than those made with the first ribbon.

5 With the last ribbon make the smallest loops.

6 Make half the loops then make a center loop by bringing the ribbon toward you-up, over and around your thumb.

7 Continue making the rest of the loops with the last ribbon. Fold a 6" piece of cloth covered wire or chenille stem in half and insert through the center loops.

8 Bring the wire ends to the back of the bow and twist to secure the ribbons.

General Directions

3

BOUQUET HOLDERS: Two types of holders are used in this book--styrofoam® and Sahara®. The styrofoam® is a firmer substance and is used when dried filler is not to be incorporated into the bouquet design or when a "whiter" look is desired. When dried materials are used in the bouquet, it is best to use a Sahara® holder. The 2 1/2" width Sahara® holder should be used as any larger size is difficult to cover and hide in the finished bouquet. Do not try to hold a bouquet as you are working on it for it is possible that the bouquet will be off balance. Either place it in a commercial stand or in an empty pop bottle as you work.

TO REINFORCE OR LENGTHEN FLOWER STEMS: Use the 20 gauge wire that comes in 18" lengths, often called stem wire. Lay a piece of this wire next to the original flower stem, just under the flower head. Twist the flower stem with your left hand while stretching the tape with your right hand. Wrap the tape snugly all the way to the end of the stem.

CRAFT GLUE: Before inserting any flowers into the foam, cut the stems at an angle and dip the cut ends in tacky craft glue. Then insert into the bouquet, this way the flowers will not twist or turn in the arrangement.

ANGLE OF FLOWER STEMS: In all bouquet styles, the flower stems should angle into the center of the holder as shown below.

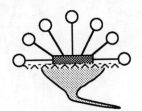 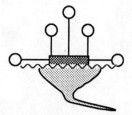

Like this   not this

HOW TO CORRECTLY HOLD A BOUQUET: Place the index and middle finger of your right hand in front of the bouquet handle. The other three fingers should be behind the handle. Your left hand should rest comfortably over your right hand which is on the bouquet handle. See the drawings below, the bouquet is not held at the waist but in a lower, more relaxed, position.

Like this   not this

Cascade Bouquet Basics

A full or slim cascade is perfect for the bride or her maids. Traditionally the maids' cascades are a bit shorter than the bride's. The cascade will be a length of ivy or similar trailing material. With floral tape, add flowers that are in the upper portion of the bouquet to this cascade piece. Dip the stem into glue and insert into the center bottom of the foam holder, let dry.

The following placements determine if the bouquet will be full or slim. The further the flowers are away from the holder, the fuller the bouquet will be. Insert a 4"-6" piece at a spot between 1:00 and 2:00 into the foam. This piece will rest on the left forearm when the bouquet is correctly held (see the drawing on page 3). Add a third piece in direct line with the second piece on the other side of the bouquet. Insert two more pieces equally spaced into the top left side of the bouquet. Finally a small piece is placed between the cascade and #2 piece, at about the 4:00 or 5:00 position.

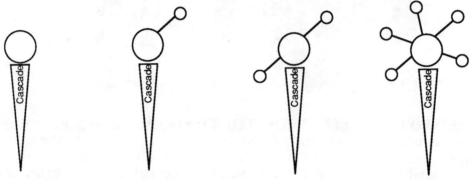

Insert the largest, fullest, prettiest flower into the center of the bouquet. If there is enough space, add another flower in a line from #2 to the center flower and from the center flower to the cascade.

Insert one flower to connect each point to the center flower. Then tuck in any flowers as needed to fill the space between flowers and to establish the outline of the bouquet.

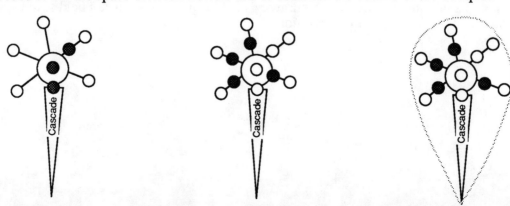

Peach & Blue Slim Cascade

YOU WILL NEED:

4" wide styrofoam® bouquet holder
5 1/2 yards of 3/4" wide white lace
    ribbon
5 1/2 yards of 3/4" wide double-faced
    satin peach ribbon
5 1/2 yards of 3/8" wide double-faced
    satin light blue ribbon
2 stems green ivy (each stem
    has an 11" piece & two 9" pieces,
    leaves vary from 1 1/2" to 3" long)
2 peach open roses, each 3" across
7 peach rosebuds, 1" tall heads
3 stems lt. blue lilies (each stem has six
    2" wide blossoms & three 1" tall
    buds)
3 stems white silk baby's breath
green floral tape
two 18" pieces of 20 gauge wire
1 white chenille stem (for bow)
tacky craft glue

1

2

3

4

1 Cut away the two side pieces on one ivy stem, leaving one long center piece. Cut this center piece so it is 13" long, set aside. Floral tape all roses to 3" pieces of 20 gauge wire.

2 Take one lily stem and cut off one bud and two open lilies. To form the cascade: floral tape flowers to the 13" ivy piece. Begin by taping the lily bud 2" below the tip of the ivy. Continue floral taping the open lily, baby's breath sprig, rosebud, open lily, baby's breath sprig and a rosebud.

3 Dip the end of the ivy cascade in glue. Insert into the center of the bottom edge of the styrofoam® holder.

4 Cut off a 5" stem of ivy. Insert into the #2 location (see cascade basics, page 4) between the 1:00 and 2:00 positions on the styrofoam® holder.

6

5

6

5 Cut four 5" pieces of ivy. Following the directions on page 4, insert these pieces into positions #3, #4, #5 and #6.

6 Insert one open rose into the center of the bouquet.

7

8

7 Cut off three lily pieces, each should contain a bud and one open blossom. Insert one piece in front of positions #2, #3 and #6.

8 Insert one rosebud in front of positions #4 and #5.

9

10

9 See the directions on page 2 to make two many ribboned bows. Each bow will have 10 loops. The longest loops are 4". Insert one bow on each side of the center rose.

10 For streamers: cut two 36" lengths of each ribbon and lace. Place together and fold in half. Insert a 6" piece of wire over the fold and twist to the ends. Insert next to the cascade. Insert the second open rose under the first. Angle the stem up into the bouquet.

11

12

11 Randomly insert the remaining roses and lilies to fill the empty spaces. The lily buds should extend 1" beyond the roses in the bouquet.

12 Cut the baby's breath into single sprigs. Insert them throughout the bouquet extending 1"-2" beyond the roses. Three larger ivy leaves are removed from the stems and glued into the ribbon around the center of the bouquet. Insert the remaining ivy pieces throughout the bouquet.

Mauve & Ivory Full Cascade

YOU WILL NEED:

*one 2 1/2" wide Sahara® bouquet
    holder*
*8 yards of 1 1/2" wide ivory lace
    ribbon*
*8 yards of 5/8" wide ivory double
    faced satin ribbon*
1 orchid cascade
7 mauve satin lilies (each 5" wide)
3 mauve satin lily buds (each 2 1/2" tall)
*9 orchid picks (these are purchased with
    each pick having one 3" wide orchid
    and 3 stephanotis blossoms)*
cloth covered wire or chenille stem
green floral tape
tacky craft glue

1

2

1 To complete the cascade, floral tape one
lily bud so the tip is 2" from the end of
the cascade. Notice 1"-2" of the lily
stem is not floral taped.

2 Floral tape an open lily half way up the
cascade.

3

4

3 Cut the cascade stem to 1" long. Dip the
end into glue and insert into the center
bottom of the bouquet holder. Let dry
overnight.

4 Cut five orchid stems to 1" long and
insert for each of the five outer
placements as shown on page 4.

5

6

5 Cut one open lily stem to 3" long. Insert into the center of the foam.

6 Insert one lily bud in front of the flower in placement #2 at the upper right of the bouquet.

7

8

7 Insert one lily bud between #4 and #5, at the upper left side.

8 Insert one open lily in the upper left and one in the upper right. These will connect the ouside buds with the center flower.

9

10

9 Insert one open lily in front of the orchid pick at positions #3 and #6.

10 Insert one open lily directly below the center lily to connect it with the cascade.

11

12

11 Insert the remaining four orchid picks around the outside center of the bouquet to fill in the space.

12 Follow the directions on page 2 to make a bow with the satin and lace ribbons. Each bow has ten 3" long loops. For streamers: fold a 36" length each of satin and lace ribbon in half. Place the fold behind the bow and secure with the bow wire. Repeat making a second bow and streamer. Insert one to the left and one to the right of the center flower.

Crescent Bouquet Basics

This beautiful bouquet is best when used with a gown which has a very detailed front. You can either use a ready-made cascade base such as a length of ivy or you can floral tape flowers together to create the cascade look. To begin, use a 4" length of floral tape to attach a flower to the tip of the cascade. Be sure to pull the tape tight so the flower does not loosen and fall off. The next flower is taped in place and angled slightly to the left. Be sure to leave space between the flowers. Smaller filler material, like dried flowers or small silks, are taped to the stem between the main flowers. The next flower is taped and angled slightly to the right. Continue adding flowers and alternating the angle. If there are very large flowers in the main bouquet, such as large roses or gardenias, use these only at the top of the cascade.

When complete, gently curve the cascade and glue it into the center of the right side of the foam. Make another cascade about 1/3 to 1/2 the length of the first. Gently curve it and glue into the left side of the foam. Insert a flower into the center of the foam. Then insert two flowers into the foam, these will connect the center flower to each cascade.

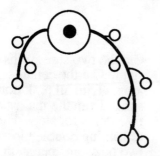 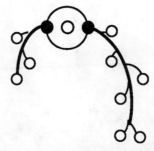

Insert flowers around the top and bottom of the bouquet to form a small oval. Then add flowers forming another row between the top and the center rows. Stagger these flowers with those already in the bouquet.

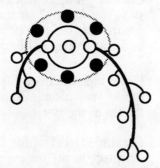 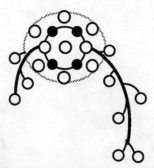

Make a bow and insert into the center of the bouquet. Bring the streamers down each cascade and, with pieces of cloth covered wire, attach the streamers to the cascades in several places. Tuck in filler flowers and greens to fill the center section of the bouquet.

Burgundy Short Crescent Cascade

YOU WILL NEED:

2 1/2" wide Sahara® bouquet holder
1 stem burgundy lilies (it has 6 flowers, each 2" wide, and two buds)
2 stems green ivy (each stem has an 11" piece and two 9" pieces. Leaves vary from 1 1/2"--3")
8 mauve rosebuds, each 1 1/2" tall
2 stems pink double blossoms (each stem has 6 sprigs of four 3/4" wide flowers)
3 yards of 3/4" wide pink/white lace ribbon
white cloth covered wire
green floral tape
20 gauge wire in 18" lengths
6 wooden picks
chenille stem for bow
tacky craft glue

1

3

2

4

1   Cut the two side sprigs off one ivy stem. Cut the center stem so it is 12" long. Trim all pink double blossom sprigs from the main stems. Set aside five stems for steps 4 and 6. Cut the remaining double blossoms so there are two blossoms per stem. Floral tape each stem to a 2" length of wire. Set aside for step 12.

2   Cut one group of lilies from the main stem leaving a 1" stem on the cut group. Cut off two open lilies leaving a bud and one open lily on the stem.

3   Floral tape the open lily and bud stem to the 12" ivy piece. Place the bud near the tip of the ivy.

4   Continue floral taping flowers along the ivy piece in the following order: double blossom, rosebud, double blossom, open lily, rosebud and double blossom. Gently curve the stem.

5

6

7

8

9

10

11

12

5 Cut the ivy stem to 2" long. Dip the cut end in glue and insert into the right side of the holder, as shown.

6 Cut an 8" length of ivy. Floral tape flowers to the ivy in the following order (beginning at the tip of the ivy): lily bud, double blossom, rosebud and double blossom. Cut the ivy stem to 1" long. Gently curve the stem.

7 Dip the cut end of the ivy into glue and insert into the left side of the holder.

8 Cut the rosebud stems to 2" long. Insert one rosebud into the center of the foam.

9 Cut four more rosebud stems to 2" long. Insert two around the top of the holder and two around the bottom of the holder. These will visually "connect" the two cascades.

10 Follow the directions on page 1 and make a bow with 12" and 18" streamers. The bow should have 14 loops, each 2" long. Insert the bow into the center of the holder with a streamer down each ivy piece. With pieces of cloth covered wire, secure each streamer to the ivy cascade in a few spots.

11 Cut off four open lilies and floral tape each to a 2" length of wire. Insert around the center rose, see the photo for placement. Glue small ivy leaves into the ribbon loops in the center of the bow.

12 For two loop picks: make 2 loops each 2" long. Place a wooden pick over the folds and wrap securely with the wire. Make 6 picks and insert around the sides of the bouquet. Insert the double blossom sprigs throughout the bouquet.

Rose & Pearl Crescent

YOU WILL NEED:

4" wide styrofoam® bouquet holder
27 white rosebuds, each 1 1/2" long
36 pearl sprays, each with 3 strands
of pearls
4 yards of 7/8" wide white iridescent
ribbon
4 pieces of 20 gauge wire, each 18"
long
white cloth covered wire
green floral tape
chenille stem for bow
tacky craft glue

1 Cut 3 rosebud stems so they are 3" long and set aside for steps 7 and 9. Cut the other rosebud stems to 2" then floral tape one pearl spray about 1" below the head of each rosebud.

2 Floral tape two pieces of the 20 gauge wire together. Tape a rosebud to one end.

3 Floral tape a second rosebud so the head is about 1" below the head of the first and angle it to the right. When floral taping these flowers to the stem, begin 1" below the head of the flower.

4 Floral tape another rosebud about 1" below the head of the second. Angle it to the left.

WHITE FAN

You Will Need:
16"x8" white lace fan
5 yards of 5/8" wide white iridescent striped ribbon
5 yards of 1 1/2" wide white lace ribbon
1 stem white open orchids (with ten 3" wide flowers and 2 buds)
2 stems ivy (about 18 leaves from 1 1/2" to 2 1/2" long)
24 pearl stems, each with 3 strands
cloth covered wire
tacky craft glue

See page 12 for directions.

SHORT WHITE CASCADE

You Will Need:
2 1/2" wide Sahara® bouquet holder
13 white rosebuds, each bud 2" long
1 stem green/white ivy, with about 50 leaves each 2" long
3 yards of 1 1/2" wide white lace ribbon
3 yards of 5/8" wide white satin ribbon
tacky craft glue

ALL WHITE WREATH

You Will Need:
14" styrofoam® wreath
1 stem ivy with 18 leaves from 1 1/2" to 2 1/2" long
1 stem white orchids with ten 3" wide flowers and two buds
2 white doves
4 yards of 1 1/2" sheer iridescent lacedge ribbon
4 yards of 1/2" wide iridescent ribbon
6 1/2 yards of 1 1/2" wide white moire ribbon (to wrap the wreath)
pole pins
glue gun & hot glue or tacky craft glue

14

TEAL & RASPBERRY SHORT CRESCENT

You Will Need:
2 1/2" wide Sahara® holder
11" vine heart wreath
8 yards of 5/8" wide primrose edge lace ribbon
8 yards of 3/8" wide teal picot ribbon
18 ivy leaves, each 1 1/2" to 2 1/2" long
8 sprigs teal double blossoms (each sprig has four 3/4" wide
    flowers)
1 pink/raspberry alstromeria stem (seven 2" wide flowers and
    many buds per stem)
four 2" wide open white roses and three 1" long buds (1 stem)
cloth covered wire
glue gun & hot glue or tacky craft glue

TEAL & RASPBERRY MINI FAN

You Will Need:
4"x8" white lace fan
2 pink carnations, each 2" across
2 pink rosebuds, each 2" tall
2 sprigs teal double blossoms (four 3/4" wide blossoms per
    sprig)
2 yards of 5/8" wide raspberry edged white lace ribbon
2 yards of 3/8" wide teal picot ribbon
cloth covered wire

See page 25 for directions.

PEACH AND BLUE PARASOL

You Will Need:
white lace parasol
32 blue rosebuds, each bud 1 1/2" long
16 sprigs peach double blossoms (each sprig with four 3/4" wide
    blossoms)
8 sprigs of silk white baby's breath (1 stem)
32 green/white ivy leaves (1 stem, each leaf 2" long)
8 yards of 5/8" wide double faced peach satin ribbon
8 yards of 3/8" wide double faced peach satin ribbon
16 yards of 3/8" wide double faced blue satin ribbon
8 yards of 5/8" wide white lace ribbon
cloth covered wire
glue gun & hot glue or tacky craft glue

See page 5 for directions.

PEACH & BLUE WREATH   See page 19 for directions.

You Will Need:
5/8"x12" styrofoam® ring
5 1/2 yards of 1 1/2" wide peach moire ribbon (to wrap)
1 1/2 yards of 5/8" wide white lace ribbon (to twist)
1 1/2 yards of 3/8" wide blue scalloped edge ribbon (to twist)
5 yards of 5/8" wide white lace ribbon (for bows)
5 yards of 3/8" wide blue scalloped edge ribbon (for bows)
5 yards of 3/8" wide peach double faced satin ribbon (for bows)
5 peach open roses, each 2 1/2" wide
10 sprigs blue double blossoms (each sprig has four 3/4" wide
    flowers)
15 green ivy leaves, each 1 1/2" wide (1 stem)
glue gun & hot glue or tacky craft glue

BLUE CLOSED PARASOL

You Will Need:
1 white lace parasol
1 corsage wristlet
2 light blue open roses, each 3" wide
6 light blue rosebuds, each bud 2" long
1 stem royal blue starburst flowers (each stem has 4 sections of six 1" wide flowers)
illusion galaxy gyp (iridescent baby's breath)
3 yards of 5/8" wide royal iridescent striped ribbon
3 yards of 3/8" wide iridescent ribbon
green floral tape
cloth covered wire

See page 21 for directions.

BLUE FAN VARIATION

You Will Need:
11"x7" white lace fan with Sahara® holder
8 royal blue rosebuds, each bud 1 1/2" long
7 light blue rosebuds, each bud 1 1/2" long
illusion galaxy gyp (iridescent baby's breath)
2 yards of 1/2" wide iridescent royal striped ribb
2 yards of 1/2" wide iridescent ribbon
white cloth covered wire

BLUE CRESCENT BOUQUET

You Will Need:
2 1/2" wide Sahara® holder
14 light blue rosebuds, each bud 2" tall
3 medium blue open roses, each 1 1/2" wide
2 medium blue rosebuds, each bud 2 1/2" tall
illusion galaxy gyp (iridescent baby's breath)
4 yards of 5/8" wide royal blue iridescent striped ribbon
4 yards of 3/8" wide iridescent ribbon
cloth covered wire
18" lengths of 20 gauge wire
green floral tape

5

6

7

8

9

10

11

12

17

5 Repeat steps 3 and 4 with five more rosebuds. Cut the remaining stem so it is 3" below the last rosebud. Gently curve the stem. Glue it into the center of the right side of the holder.

6 Repeat steps #2--#4 to form another cascade using four flowers. Cut the wire leaving a 1" stem. Gently curve the stem and glue into the center of the left side of the holder.

7 Take one rosebud with a 3" stem and insert it into the center of the styrofoam®, 2" of the stem will show.

8 Following the directions on page 1, make a bow with fourteen 3" long loops and one 12" and one 26" streamer. Insert the bow into the center of the holder under the center rosebud. With cloth covered wire attach the 12" streamer down the left cascade in two places. Attach the 26" streamer down the right cascade in four places.

9 Take two rosebuds with 3" stems and insert one on each side of the center rose. Angle the stems into the center. These will "connect" a line between the two cascades.

10 Insert four rosebuds around the top of the bouquet to "connect" the cascades. And insert three rosebuds around the bottom of the bouquet.

11 Insert three rosebuds between the center and the top row. Repeat inserting two rosebuds between the center and bottom row.

12 Cut the pearl stems to 1" long. Randomly insert them to fill in the design.

Fan Basics

Fan bouquets give a beautiful accent to any wedding. There are two popular fan styles--the mound and the S-curve. The lace fan you choose will need to have a Sahara® holder.

MOUND STYLE: (1) Insert one flower straight up into the center of the foam.
(2) Add three flowers in a semi-circle to create a second row.

1   **2**

(3) Insert four more flowers in another semi-circle creating a third row. This row should rest on the lace fan. (4) Insert another type of flower as shown by the X's in the diagram. These flowers should be different from the first flowers in color and texture. You can use rosebuds and carnations or lilies and carnations as each of these combinations is very different in texture.

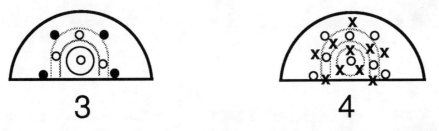

3   **4**

S-CURVE: (1) Lay the fan on the table and insert one flower straight up into the center of the foam. The flower should extend no more than a few inches from the foam. (2) Gently curve the stems of two more flowers and insert these into the foam at the upper left and lower right of the foam. The lower right flower will cascade over the edge of the fan.

1   **2**

(3) Gently curve the stems of two more flowers and insert into the left and right of the foam. These flowers will extend the "S" which is being formed. (4) Insert another type of flower as shown by the X's in the diagram. These flowers should be different in color and texture from the first flowers.

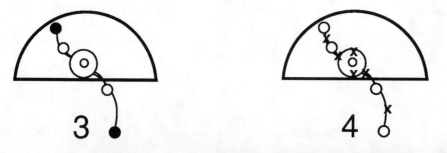

3   **4**

Peach & Blue Mound Fan

YOU WILL NEED:

9"x14" white lace fan with Sahara® holder
4 stems blue lilies (each stem has two groups of three 2" wide flowers and one bud)
10 peach rosebuds, each 1 1/2" long
2 stems white silk baby's breath
3 yards 1/2" wide white lace ribbon
3 yards 1/2" wide peach double faced satin ribbon
3 yards 3/8" wide light blue double faced satin ribbon
chenille stem for bow
white cloth covered wire
tacky craft glue

1

2

1 Cut all lily stems apart into two sections. Cut each lily stem to 1" long. Cut all rosebud stems to 4" long. Following the basic directions on page 18, insert the lilies into the main flower locations.

2 Insert the rosebuds into the secondary flower locations. Notice they are pressed deeper into the arrangement than the lily buds.

3

4

3 Cut the baby's breath sprigs off the main stem. Insert them randomly throughout to fill the bouquet.

4 Following the directions on page 2, make a many ribboned bow. Measure 18" from the end of each ribbon or lace before making the bow. Begin with the peach ribbon, then use the lace and finally the blue ribbon. All bows have 8 loops, each 3"-4" long.

Mauve "S" Fan

YOU WILL NEED:

*7"x11" white lace fan with Sahara®
    holder
11 pink rosebuds, each 1 1/2" long
2 stems mauve double blossoms (each
    stem has 6 sprigs of four 3/4" wide
    flowers)
5 yards 1/2" wide pink/white lace
    ribbon
3 yards 1/8" burgundy satin ribbon
green floral tape
white cloth covered wire
20 gauge wire in 18" lengths
chenille stems for bows
wooden picks
tacky craft glue*

1   Following the basic directions for the
"S" curve on page 18, steps 1 and 2,
insert three 3" rosebuds into the holder.
Cut 2 rosebuds to 6" and place as
shown in step 3 of the basic directions.
The last six rosebuds are 3" long and
go around the center rosebud.

2   Following the directions on page 1,
make a 14 loop bow with 12" streamers
out of the lace ribbon. Each loop is 2"
long. Insert the bow under the center
rosebud. Using pieces of cloth covered
wire, secure the lace streamers up and
down the "S."

1

2

3   Cut the remaining lace ribbon into two
1 yard pieces. See page 1 to make two
bows, each with eight 2" long loops.
Insert into each side of the foam. Cut 8
double blossom sprigs (each with 4
flowers) off the center stem. Insert at
each end of the design.

4   Cut remaining blossoms so there are 2
flowers per stem. Insert around the
center rosebud. See page 11, step 12
and make double loops with the 1/8"
ribbon. Floral tape over the wire. Glue
into the bouquet following the curve.
Leave a 5" streamer on the bottom set
of loops.

3

4

Wreath Bouquet

YOU WILL NEED:

12" wide by 1/2" thick styrofoam® ring
5 yards 1 1/2" wide white iridescent
  ribbon
10 royal blue starburst flowers, each
  1 1/2" across
5 light blue rosebuds, each 1 1/2" long
12 white stephanotis, 1 1/2" wide
white sparkling baby's breath (Illusion
  Galaxy Gyp)
6 yards 5/8" wide royal blue iridescent
  striped ribbon
6 yards 1/2" wide white iridescent
  ribbon
pearl headed boutonniere straight pins
white floral tape
white cloth covered wire
glue gun & hot glue

**The bride or bridesmaid holds this
wreath between the top two bows
and carries it down at her side.**

1 Black pins are used
  in the photos.

1   Wrap the styrofoam® ring with 1 1/2"
  ribbon. Insert two pins 4" apart on one
  side of the wreath. Between these pins
  will be where the wreath is held by the
  bridesmaid.

2   Cut off 1 1/2 yards each of iridescent
  and striped iridescent ribbons. Place
  together and pin one end to the ring next
  to one pin. Wrap the ribbons through
  and around the ring twisting each ribbon
  separately as you go. Pin as necessary.

3   Repeat wrapping and twisting the
  ribbons, pin to the ring every 6 3/4".
  There will be six pinned spots. Do not
  twist any ribbon between the 4" space.

4   Cut off six 27" lengths of iridescent
  and striped iridescent ribbons. See
  page 2 to make six bows of each ribbon.
  Each striped bow will have six 2" long
  loops. Top each striped bow with an
  iridescent bow with six 2" long loops.
  Save the bows for step 8.

3

4

2

5

6

5 Hold together two royal starburst flowers and two stephanotis flowers. Add several 2"–4" long sprigs of baby's breath and floral tape together.

6 Place a rosebud in the center, add more baby's breath, and floral tape together. Cut the stems to 1/2" long.

7

8

7 Repeat steps 5 and 6 to make a total of five bundles.

8 Use hot glue to attach a floral bundle over the first pin spot as shown.

9

10

9 Place the next four bundles each at a pin spot as pictured.

10 Hot glue a double bow (from step 4) over the stems of each floral bundle.

11

12

11 Hot glue the last double bow over the last pin spot.

12 Cut one stephanotis off the stem and glue into the last bow. Cut off 3" lengths of baby's breath. Dip the cut ends in glue and add to this last bow.

Grapevine Wreath Bouquet

YOU WILL NEED:

10" grapevine wreath
*1 1/2 yards burgundy wired satin
   tubing*
*3 1/3 yards of 5/8" wide mauve edged
   ivory lace ribbon*
*3 1/3 yards of 1/2" wide burgundy
   picot ribbon*
7 pink rosebuds, each 1 1/2" tall
*1 stem mauve double blossoms (each
   stem has 6 sprigs of four 3/4" wide
   flowers)*
*1 stem green ivy, there is one 11" piece
   and two 9" pieces*
white cloth covered wire
green floral tape
masking tape
glue gun and hot glue

1

2

1 Cut the satin tubing into three pieces
each 18" long. Twist a 2" piece of cloth
covered wire around all three ends and
secure to the table with masking tape.
Braid the pieces and bind the other ends
with cloth covered wire.

2 Bring the ends of the tubing together
and floral tape them. Glue to the top of
the wreath as shown.

3

4

3 Cut the three pieces of ivy off the stem.
Cut all rosebuds so the stems are 3"
long. Cut all double blossoms off the
main stem just below the leaf.

4 With each shorter ivy piece: floral tape a
double blossom sprig near the tip of the
stem. Then floral tape a rosebud,
another double blossom and finish by
taping another rosebud, as shown.

5

6

5 Gently curve the two shorter ivy pieces.

6 Glue one piece to the top right side of the wreath . Glue the other piece to the top left side of the wreath.

7

8

7 For the longest ivy piece: repeat step 4 then add another rosebud at the end. Cut the stem just after the last ivy leaf.

8 Glue the longest ivy piece cascading down the center of the wreath.

9

10

9 Follow the directions on page 2 to make a bow. With the burgundy ribbon make a 10 loop bow with each loop 2 1/2" long and 12" streamers. Repeat, using the lace ribbon to make another bow with the same size loops and streamers.

10 Wire and glue the bow over the ivy ends.

11

12

11 Place one pair of 12" streamers on each side of the wreath. Use 3" pieces of cloth covered wire to secure the ribbons in two spots to each ivy stem.

12 Cut two 18" lengths of each ribbon. Hold the four ends together and glue under the center bow. Separate the ribbons and drape them around the center ivy piece. Secure in a couple of spots with pieces of cloth covered wire.

Full Parasol

YOU WILL NEED:

white lace parasol
4 stems raspberry lilies (each stem has 2 groups of three 2" wide flowers and one bud)
8 pink carnations, each 2" wide
3 stems teal blue double blossoms (each stem has 6 sprigs of four 3/4" wide flowers)
32 green/white ivy leaves, 2" long
10 yards of 3/4" wide mauve double faced satin ribbon
16 yards of 3/4" wide mauve edged white lace ribbon
16 yards of 1/4" wide teal feather edged (picot) ribbon
white cloth covered wire
green floral tape
tacky craft glue

1

2

1 Cut off a sprig of ivy with 3 leaves. Cut off one lily group then cut off one lily blossom and set aside. Place the 2 lilies and bud on top of the ivy sprig and floral tape all stems together.

2 Cut off one sprig of double blossoms and floral tape over the ivy and lily sprigs.

3

4

3 Cut a carnation stem to 2" long. Floral tape it on top of the double blossom sprig.

4 See the directions on page 2 to make a triple bow. Use four 2" loops of mauve satin ribbon, four 2" loops of mauve edged lace, and eight 1 1/2" loops of teal blue ribbon.

5

6

5 Attach a bow to the floral cluster with cloth covered wire. Repeat steps 1 through 5 to make a total of eight clusters.

6 Using a piece of cloth covered wire (which goes through the lace) attach a floral cluster to the parasol at the end of each rib as shown.. Twist the wire ends on the underside of the parasol. Repeat in a second spot on each cluster. Contine attaching all the clusters.

7

8

7 Floral tape together an ivy leaf, one lily, and one double blossom sprig.

8 Follow the directions on page 2 to make a double bow. Make one bow with four 2" long loops of the mauve edged lace ribbon. Top with a teal bow containing eight 1 1/2" long loops.

9

10

9 Secure the bow to the cluster made in step 7.

10 With cloth covered wire secure the bow and cluster to the center prong of the parasol. The bow should be toward the outer rim of the parasol.

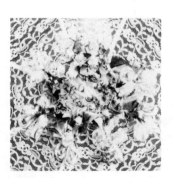

11

12

11 Repeat steps 7 through 10 making a total of 8 clusters and attach to the parasol center.

12 Use the rest of the ribbons and lace to make a large floppy bow, see page 2. The loops will be 6" long beginning with the mauve ribbon then the lace and finally using the teal ribbon. Secure to the inside of the parasol handle.

Closed Parasol

YOU WILL NEED:

white lace parasol
1 stem pink roses with two 3" wide
  open roses and one 1 1/2" tall bud
1 stem burgundy lilies with two groups
  of three 2" wide lilies and one bud
1 stem mauve double blossoms with
  6 sprigs of four 3/4" wide flowers
one wristlet (bracelet used for wrist
  corsages)
2 yards of 3/4" wide mauve double
  faced satin ribbon
2 yards of 1/2" wide burgundy
  scalloped-edge satin ribbon
2 yards of 1 1/2" wide pink/white lace
  ribbon
white cloth covered wire
green floral tape

1 Cut all roses off the main stem leaving each with a 1" wired stem.

2 Cut the double blossom stem so there are two pieces containing two sprigs and two pieces containing one sprig.

3 Cut the lily stem into two groups, each having a 1" long stem.

4 Place a double blossom stem with two sprigs behind the rosebud. Floral tape the stems together.

5

6

5 Place a lily stem on top. Floral tape all the stems together.

6 Place an open rose below the lily. Floral tape all stems together.

7

8

7 Floral tape the last double blossom below the rose.

8 Make another cluster by joining flowers in the following order: one double blossom sprig, lily stem, open rose, and one double blossom sprig.

9

10

9 Bring the ends of each floral cluster together and overlap on the wristlet clip. Bend the clips over the stems to hold them together.

10 Slip the wristlet over the closed parasol.

11

12

11 Follow the directions on page 2 to make a "many ribboned" bow. Make six 2 1/2" to 4" loops on each of the three ribbons and leave 10" tails on each bow.

12 Secure to the front of the parasol between the flower clusters.